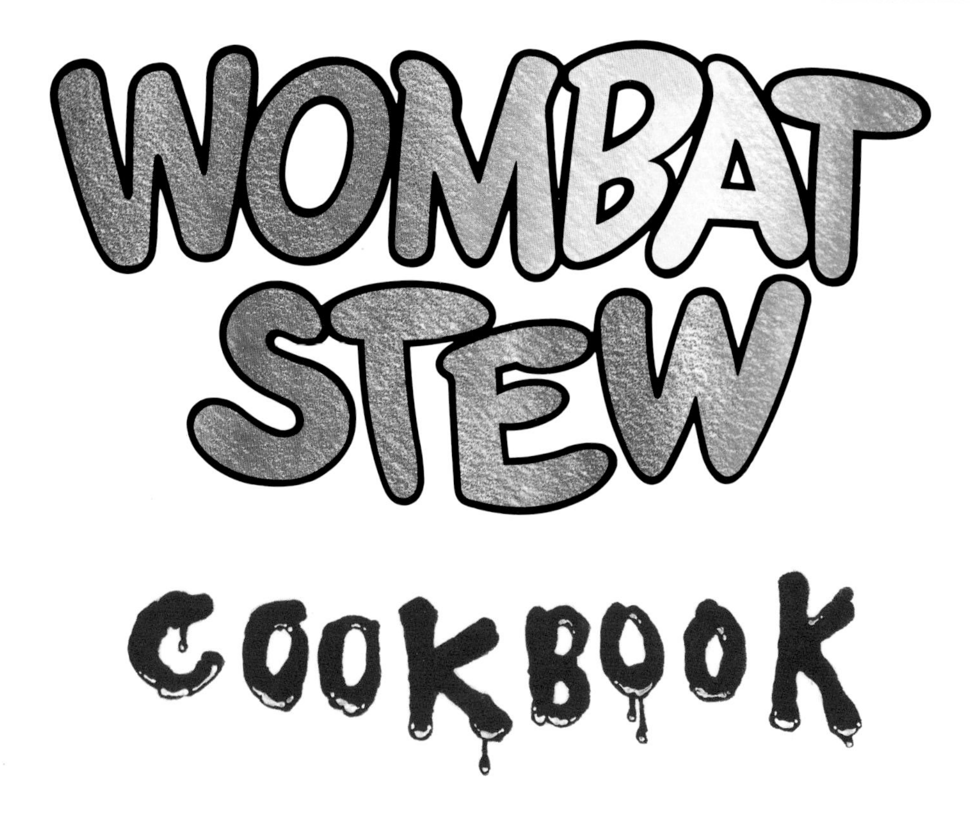

COOKBOOK

Marcia Vaughan

Illustrated by
Pamela Lofts

ASHTON SCHOLASTIC
SYDNEY AUCKLAND NEW YORK TORONTO LONDON

To Rosie . . .

PL

This book is dedicated to Mother Nature and all her friends!

My special thanks to the students of Blessed Sacrament School in Mosman, NSW, who tested these recipes with delicious results.

MV

Vaughan, Marcia K. (Marcia Kay).
Wombat stew cookbook.

ISBN 0 86896 444 1 (pbk.).
ISBN 0 86896 443 3.

1. Cookery—Juvenile literature. I. Lofts, Pamela. II. Title.

641.5'123

First published in 1989 by Ashton Scholastic Pty Limited A.C.N. 000 614 577, PO Box 579, Gosford 2250. Also in Brisbane, Melbourne, Adelaide, Perth and Auckland, NZ.

Reprinted in 1990, 1991 and 1993.

Typeset in Goudy Old Style by Excel Imaging, St Leonards NSW.

Printed in Hong Kong.

12 11 10 9 8 7 6 5 4 3 4 5 6 7 / 9

Contents

In the kitchen

Main dishes

Salad and vegetable dishes

Bread

Drinks

Desserts

In the kitchen

Safety in the kitchen

1 Always have an adult with you when you are in the kitchen. Ask them to help you.
2 Use oven mitts when handling hot tins and dishes.
3 When using a sharp knife be sure to slant the blade away from your fingers.

Before you cook

1 Wash your hands.
2 Put on an apron.
3 Read the recipe. If there is something you do not understand ask for help.
4 Get out all the ingredients and utensils you will need.
5 If you are using the oven, ask an adult to preheat it ahead of time.

After you cook

1 Wash all the dishes.
2 Wipe the bench or table.
3 Sweep the floor.
4 Leave the kitchen neat and clean.

Measuring small quantities

For small quantities use the Australian standard metric spoons:

1 tablespoon
1 teaspoon
½ teaspoon
¼ teaspoon

1 For dry ingredients fill the spoon and level off with a knife.
2 For liquid ingredients fill the spoon to the brim.

Measuring dry ingredients

For dry ingredients use the Australian standard metric cups:

1 cup
½ cup
¼ cup

1 Stand the cup on paper on a flat surface.
2 Spoon the ingredients into the cup.
3 Level off the top with a knife.

Measuring liquid ingredients

For liquid ingredients use the Australian standard metric jug.

1 Stand the jug on a flat surface.
2 Pour the liquid into the jug and check at eye level.

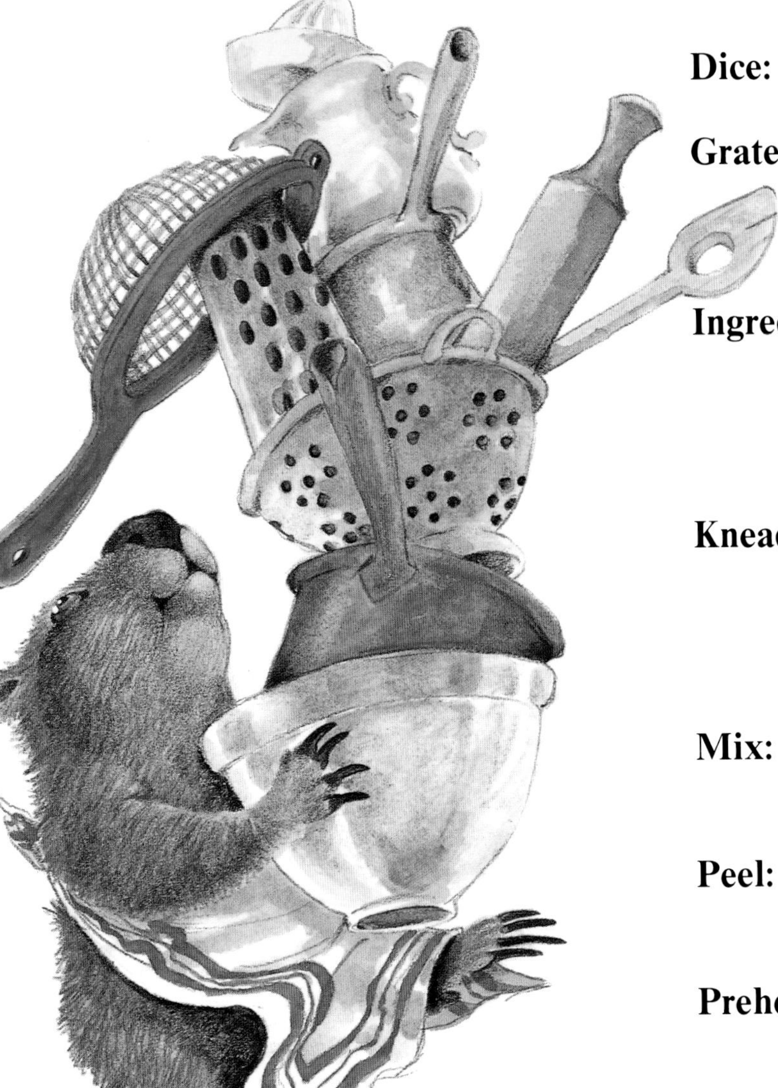

Cooking terms

Beat: To mix things using a spoon, fork or egg-beater.

Blend: To mix things well until they are smooth.

Chop: To cut something into small pieces.

Cream: To beat butter or margarine and sugar together until mixture becomes light and creamy.

Dice: To cut into small cubes.

Grate: To rub cheese or vegetable, orange or lemon peel against the side of a grater.

Ingredient: Something that goes into a mixture when you cook. Flour is an ingredient in pancakes.

Knead: To mix dough by folding, turning and pressing it away from you using the heels of your hands.

Mix: To stir or put different things together.

Peel: To remove the skin from fruits or vegetables.

Preheat: To heat an oven to the correct temperature before cooking.

Koala quick quiche

Utensils:

measuring jug, cups and spoons
large mixing bowl
paper towel
grater
knife
wooden spoon
pie or flan dish
chopping board
egg-beater
fork

Ingredients:

4 eggs
1 teaspoon oil
1 tomato
4 tablespoons sesame seeds
1 small onion
3 rashers bacon
1 teaspoon basil
1 teaspoon parsley
50 g cheese
120 ml cream
120 ml milk
1 small carrot

Method:

1 Ask an adult to preheat the oven to 190°C.
2 Break the eggs into the mixing bowl and beat them quickly with the fork until they are light and fluffy.
3 Add the cream and milk and stir with the wooden spoon until mixed.
4 Carefully chop the tomato and onion into very small pieces. Put them in the bowl.
5 Wash and peel the carrot.
6 Using the large holes in the grater, grate the carrot and put it into the bowl.
7 Carefully cut the rind from the bacon. Cut the bacon into small pieces. Put them into the bowl.
8 Now add the basil and parsley.
9 Stir 20 times to mix everything together.
10 Pour the oil into the pie dish. Using your fingertips spread the oil around until it coats the bottom and sides of the dish. Wipe your fingers on the paper towel.

11 Sprinkle the sesame seeds evenly over the bottom and sides of the dish. This will be the crust.

12 Spoon the egg mixture gently into the dish.

13 Using the large holes in the grater, grate enough cheese to fill ¼ cup.

14 Sprinkle the cheese evenly over the top of the quiche.

15 Ask an adult to place the dish into the oven and cook for 25 minutes.

16 After 25 minutes the quiche should be light brown on top and set inside. Ask an adult to check the quiche and remove it from the oven if it is ready.

17 Leave the quiche to cool for 5 minutes before serving.

Quick quiche is delicious served hot or cold.

Platypus pancakes

Utensils:

2 mixing bowls
measuring cups and spoons
wooden spoon
eggslice
electric frypan
egg-beater
knife
plate
piece of paper the size of your hand

Ingredients:

1 cup flour
1 tablespoon caster sugar
1 teaspoon bicarbonate of soda
¼ teaspoon baking powder
¼ teaspoon salt
1 egg
2 tablespoons oil
1 cup buttermilk*
butter
jam
extra oil
honey
icing sugar

* To make buttermilk stir ¼ teaspoon vinegar into 1 cup milk.

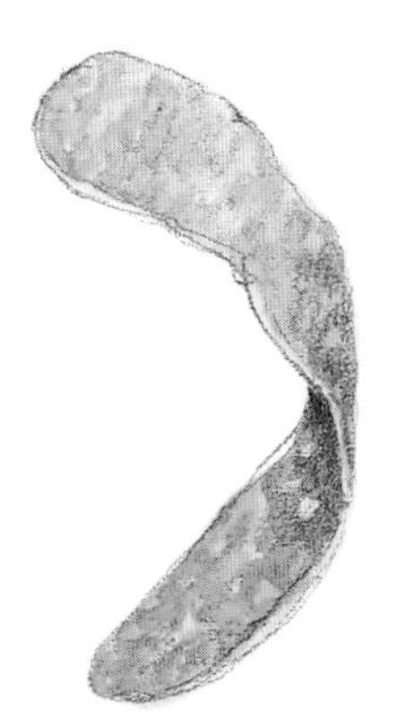

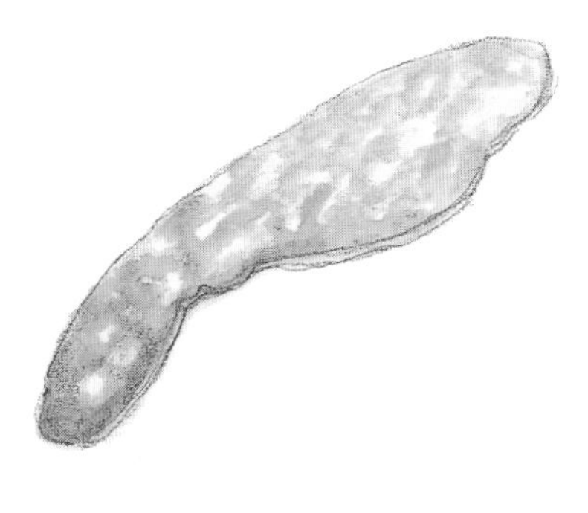

Method:

1 Measure the flour, sugar, soda, baking powder and salt into a mixing bowl. Stir 20 times with a wooden spoon.

2 Break the egg into the other bowl and beat until there is some froth on top.

3 Add the buttermilk and oil to the egg and stir until the mixture is all one colour.

4 Now add the dry ingredients to the wet ingredients. Use the egg-beater to mix them together until the batter is smooth.

5 Ask an adult to pour a little oil into the frypan. Using the piece of paper, spread the oil evenly over the surface of the pan.

6 Ask an adult to turn the heat button to a medium setting.

7 Ask an adult to help you pour ⅛ cup of batter into the hot pan and let it cook for 1 minute.

8 After 1 minute ask an adult to help you use the eggslice to turn the pancake over. Let it cook for another minute. The pancake should be golden brown on both sides.

9 Use the eggslice to place the pancake on a plate.

10 Spread the pancake with butter and top with golden syrup, maple syrup, jam, honey or icing sugar.

11 Make as many pancakes as you can, until the batter is gone.

12 If you like, you can ask an adult to put the pancakes on a tray in a warm oven. Share them with your family or friends.

Potoroo peppy pizzas

Utensils:

measuring spoons
mixing bowl
chopping board
knife
baking sheet
wooden spoon
can-opener
plates
eggslice

Ingredients:

1 packet pita bread

Sauce:

1 250 g can tomato paste
1 teaspoon brown sugar
½ teaspoon oregano
½ teaspoon onion flakes
1 teaspoon basil

Toppings:

slices of capsicum, pepperoni, salami, ham
shrimps
pineapple pieces
olives
grated cheese

Method:

1 Ask an adult to preheat the oven to 180°C.
2 Cut the toppings into slices and grate the cheese. Be careful!
3 Ask an adult to help you measure all the ingredients for the sauce into a bowl.
4 Place 2 or more pieces of pita bread next to each other on the baking sheet.
5 Spread 2 tablespoons of sauce on each pita bread.
6 Sprinkle each with cheese.
7 Arrange the toppings of your choice on top of the cheese.
8 Ask an adult to place the baking sheet near the top of the oven and let the pizzas cook for 5 to 8 minutes. The cheese and sauce should be bubbling hot.
9 When the pizzas are ready ask an adult to remove the sheet from the oven. Use the eggslice to put the pizzas onto a plate.
10 Cut each pizza into quarters.

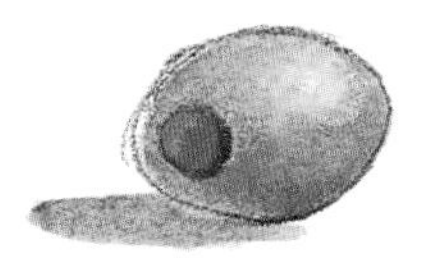

Numbat nachos

Utensils:

can-opener
knife
fork
cutting board
bowl
measuring spoon
baking sheets
eggslice
colander
serving plate
oven mitt

Ingredients:

200 g bag of corn chips
200 g cheddar cheese
440 g can baked beans
300 g carton sour cream

Method:

1. Ask an adult to preheat the oven to 200°C.
2. Arrange corn chips on the baking sheet.
3. Ask an adult to open the can of beans with a can-opener and drain the sauce through a colander.
4. Pour the beans into the bowl and mash with a fork until smooth.
5. Put 1 teaspoon of beans on each chip.
6. Carefully cut the cheese into 2 cm squares.
7. Place a square of cheese on top of each chip.
8. Ask an adult to put the tray near the top of the oven for 4 to 5 minutes or until the cheese begins to melt.
9. When the chips are ready ask an adult to remove the baking sheet from the oven. Use an eggslice to place the corn chips onto a serving plate.
10. Top each chip with a dollop of sour cream and a spoonful of Echidna avocado dip.

Crocodile soy and sesame chicken drumsticks

Utensils:

oblong baking dish
small bowl
fork
aluminium foil
measuring spoons
spoon
plate
piece of paper the size of your hand

Ingredients:

10 chicken drumsticks
3 tablespoons soy sauce
2 tablespoons honey
1 tablespoon salad oil
½ teaspoon ginger
⅛ teaspoon garlic powder
3 tablespoons sesame seeds
butter

Method:

1 Grease the baking dish by placing a pat of butter onto the piece of paper. Then, using the paper, rub the butter over the inside of the dish.
2 Place the drumsticks side by side in the baking dish.
3 Measure the soy sauce, honey, oil, ginger and garlic into a small bowl. Stir with a spoon until everything is mixed together.
4 Pour the sauce over the drumsticks. Roll the drumsticks over so that they are coated with the sauce.
5 Cover the dish with foil and chill in the refrigerator for 1 hour.
6 After 1 hour ask an adult to preheat the oven to 175°C.
7 Take the dish out of the refrigerator and remove the foil.
8 Sprinkle the sesame seeds over the drumsticks.
9 Ask an adult to place the baking dish into the oven and cook for 45 minutes.
10 After 45 minutes the drumsticks should be ready. Ask an adult to check them and remove them from the oven for you.

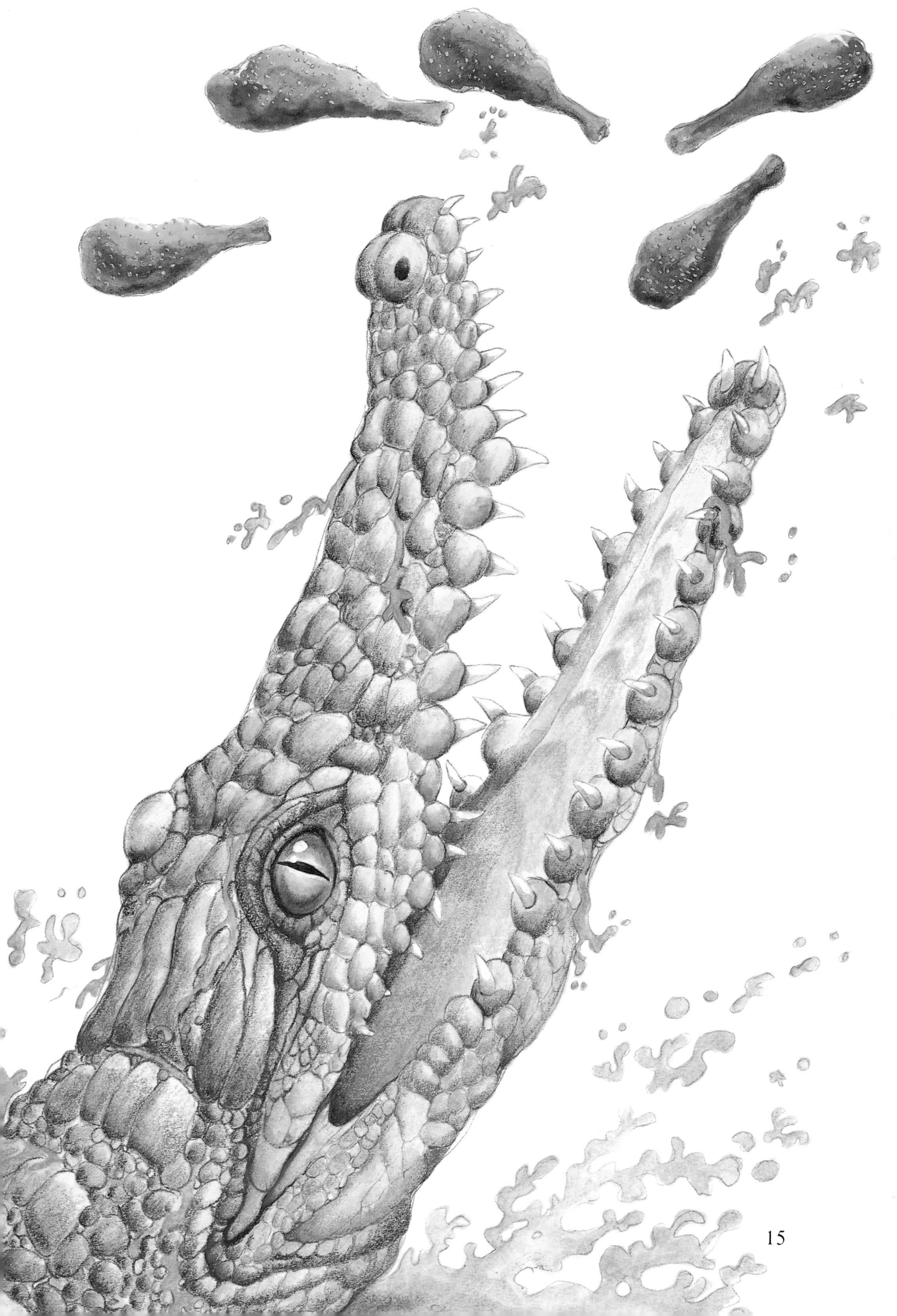

Wombat watermelon salad

Utensils:

salad plate
cutting board
knife
spoon
tea-towel

Ingredients:

lettuce leaves
1 slice of watermelon 3 cm thick
1 cup cottage cheese
strawberries

Method:

1 Wash the lettuce leaves under cold tap water, then pat them dry with the tea-towel. Arrange the lettuce on a salad plate.
2 Ask an adult to cut the watermelon into 5 wedges on the cutting board, then cut off the rind.
3 Arrange the melon wedges on the lettuce in a circle with the points facing out to make a star.
4 Spoon the cottage cheese into the centre of the star.
5 Now arrange the berries on top of the cottage cheese.

Kookaburra carrot and raisin salad

Utensils:

mixing bowl
grater
measuring cups and spoons
spoons
vegetable peeler

Ingredients:

4 tablespoons mayonnaise
2 carrots
1 cup raisins

Method:

1 Wash and peel the carrots.
2 Using the large holes in the grater, grate the carrots into the mixing bowl. Be careful not to scrape your knuckles on the grater!
3 Now measure the raisins and mayonnaise into the bowl. Stir until the carrots and raisins are coated with mayonnaise.

Echidna avocado dip

Utensils:

knife
chopping board
spoon
fork
bowl

Ingredients:

2 ripe avocados
2 tablespoons mayonnaise
4 teaspoons taco sauce

Method:

1. Cut the avocados in half. Throw away the seeds.
2. Use the spoon to scoop the avocados' flesh into the bowl. Mash with a fork until smooth.
3. Stir in the mayonnaise and the taco sauce until the mixture is one colour.
4. Use as a dip for raw vegetable slices or corn chips.

Flying fox fruit salad

Utensils:

large bowl
chopping board
knife
vegetable peeler
wooden spoon

Ingredients:

2 oranges
your favourite fresh fruits such as:
grapes
banana
peach
pear
apple
melon
kiwi fruit
berries
pawpaw
pineapple

Method:

1. Wash the fruit under the tap. Ask an adult to peel the pineapple and slice it into rings.
2. Carefully cut the fruit into small pieces. Throw away peels, seeds, pits and cores.
3. Stir the fruit pieces together in a large bowl.
4. Ask an adult to cut the oranges in half.
5. Squeeze the oranges over the fruit.
6. Stir until the fruit is coated with orange juice.
7. Chill in the refrigerator for 20 minutes before serving.

Spoonbill scones

Utensils:

measuring cups and spoons
mixing bowl
scone cutter
chopping board
rolling pin
2 saucers
pastry brush
fork
spoon
baking tray
piece of paper the size of your hand
plate

Ingredients:

2 cups self-raising flour
1 tablespoon butter
170 ml (¾ cup) milk
½ teaspoon salt
2 teaspoons sugar
extra milk
extra flour

Method:

1 Ask an adult to preheat the oven to 200°C.
2 Grease the baking tray by placing a little piece of butter on the paper. Using the paper, spread the butter over the inside of the baking tray.

3. Measure the flour, salt and sugar into the mixing bowl. Stir together 20 times so that the ingredients are all well mixed.
4. Using your fingertips and thumb rub the butter into the flour until the butter disappears.
5. Add the milk and stir quickly with a fork until you have a soft dough.
6. Put some extra flour in a saucer. Dip your hands in the flour, then rub them together so that the palms of your hands are covered with flour.
7. Sprinkle some extra flour on a board. Spoon the dough onto the flour.
8. Knead the dough by pressing it away from you with the heel of your hand. Then turn the dough over. Sprinkle some more flour on it. Fold it in half and knead it again. Do this 10 times or until the dough is smooth and firm.
9. Wipe off the board so it is not sticky. Sprinkle the board with some more flour. Rub flour on the rolling pin. Set the dough on the board. Sprinkle some flour on top of the dough.
10. Using the rolling pin roll out the dough till it is as thick as your thumbnail (1.5 cm).
11. Dip the scone cutter into the saucer of flour. Now press the scone cutter into the dough. Place the cut scone onto the baking tray. Cut all the dough in this way and arrange them on the tray. Be sure that you leave 2 cm between each scone.
12. Pour the extra milk (about ¼ cup) into the second saucer. Using the pastry brush, paint the top of each scone with a little milk.
13. Ask an adult to place the tray in the oven and cook for 10 minutes.
14. After 10 minutes the scones should be golden brown. If they are ready, ask an adult to remove the tray from the oven.
15. Let the scones cool on the tray for 3 minutes before removing to a plate.

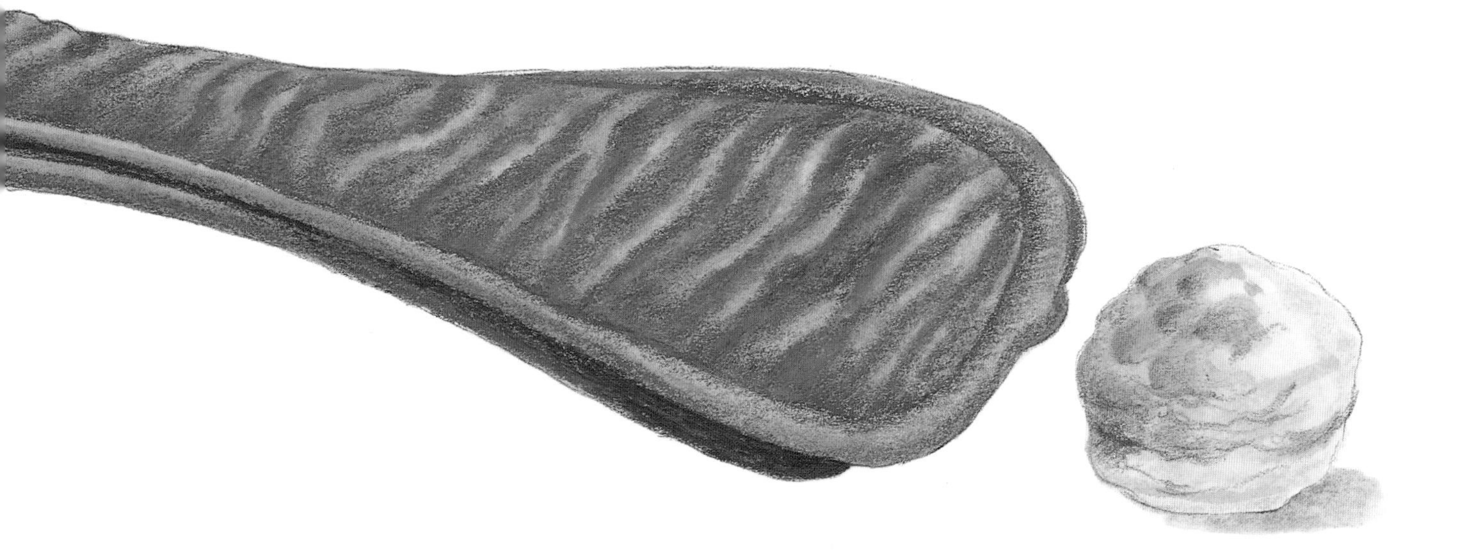

Dingo damper

Utensils:

fork
mixing bowl
spoon
measuring cups and spoons
baking sheet
piece of paper the size of your hand

Ingredients:

3 cups self-raising flour*
1 teaspoon salt
1 teaspoon sugar
250 ml milk
butter

* Equal amounts of wholemeal self-raising flour and plain self-raising flour can be used in this recipe.

Method:

1 Ask an adult to preheat the oven to 180°C.
2 Measure the flour, sugar and salt into the mixing bowl.
3 Add the milk and stir together quickly with a fork until you make a soft dough.
4 Grease the baking sheet by placing a little piece of butter onto the paper, then rub the butter all over the inside of the baking sheet.
5 Shape the dough into a ball and place it on the baking sheet.
6 Flatten the dough slightly with your hand.
7 Ask an adult to place the tray into the oven. Bake the damper for 25 minutes.
8 After 25 minutes ask an adult to help you check the damper by sticking a knife into the centre. If it comes out clean, the damper is ready. If dough sticks to the knife, bake the damper 5 minutes more, then check again.
9 When the damper is cooked, ask an adult to take it out of the oven. Let it cool on the baking sheet for 5 minutes.

Lizard lemon fizz

Utensils:

lemon squeezer
tablespoon
chopping board
knife
2 straws
tall glasses

Ingredients:

2 lemons
soda water
2 tablespoons icing sugar
ice cubes

Method:

1. Ask an adult to cut the lemons in half.
2. Squeeze the juice from 2 lemon halves into each glass.
3. Add 1 tablespoon icing sugar to each glass.
4. Put several ice cubes in each glass.
5. Fill the glasses with soda water.
6. Stir with the straw and serve right away.

Mopoke milkshake

Utensils:

large screw-top jar with lid
large spoon
measuring cups and spoons
2 glasses

Ingredients:

2 scoops vanilla ice-cream
500 ml milk
1 tablespoon icing sugar
1 teaspoon vanilla

Method:

1. Measure milk, sugar, vanilla and ice-cream into the jar. Screw the lid on tightly.
2. Hold onto the jar tightly and shake it for 1 minute (about 120 times).
3. Pour milkshake into glasses and drink right away.

Emu brew

Utensils:

chopping board
knife
large jug
tall drinking glasses
can-opener
long-handled spoon

Ingredients:

1 litre pineapple juice
1 425 ml can apricot nectar
1 litre lemonade
1 litre ginger ale
3 oranges
1 apple
mint sprigs

Method:

1 Chill the pineapple juice, apricot nectar, lemonade and ginger ale in the refrigerator.
2 Ask an adult to cut the oranges in half.
3 Squeeze the juice into a jug.
4 Carefully chop the apple into small pieces. Throw away the core.
5 Add the apple pieces to the jug.
6 Ask an adult to help you open the bottles and cans of juice and drink.
7 Carefully pour the pineapple juice, apricot nectar, lemonade and ginger ale into the jug and stir with a long-handled spoon.
8 Pour the brew into tall glasses and decorate each with a sprig of mint.

Tasmanian devil food cake

Utensils:

wooden spoon
2 mixing bowls
measuring cups and spoons
knife
20 cm x 20 cm cake pan
cooling rack
piece of paper the size of your hand
cake plate

Ingredients:

120 ml oil
225 ml milk
2 eggs
1 teaspoon vanilla
1½ cups flour
1 cup sugar
3 tablespoons cocoa or carob powder
1 teaspoon bicarbonate of soda
1 teaspoon baking soda
2 tablespoons icing sugar
butter

Method:

1. Ask an adult to preheat the oven to 180°C.
2. Break the eggs into a mixing bowl and beat lightly.
3. Add the milk, vanilla and oil. Stir 25 times with a wooden spoon.
4. In the second bowl measure the flour, sugar, cocoa, soda and baking powder. Stir 25 times.
5. Stir the dry ingredients into the wet ingredients.
6. Beat quickly for 2 minutes so that the batter is smooth and light.
7. Grease the cake pan by placing a little piece of butter on the paper. Using the paper rub the butter all over the inside of the pan.
8. Carefully pour the batter into the pan.
9. Ask an adult to put the pan into the oven and let the cake bake for 35 minutes.
10. After 35 minutes the cake should be ready. Ask an adult to remove the pan from the oven and let the cake cool for 10 minutes. If the cake is not ready let it cook 5 to 10 minutes longer.
11. When the pan is cool, run a knife around the edge of the cake. Ask an adult to help you place the cake onto the cooling rack.
12. When the cake is cool sprinkle it with icing sugar and carefully move it to a cake plate.

Possum peanut-butter balls

Utensils:

wooden spoon
2 mixing bowls
tray

Ingredients:

1 cup sesame seeds
1 cup desiccated coconut
1 cup peanut butter
½ cup honey
¼ cup instant milk powder

Method:

1. Measure the sesame seeds, coconut and powdered milk into a mixing bowl. Stir together with a wooden spoon.
2. In the second mixing bowl measure the peanut butter and honey. Stir until everything is well mixed.
3. Add a little of the dry ingredients to the peanut-butter mixture and stir together. Repeat this until all of the dry mixture has been added. Stir 25 times so that the mixture is smooth.
4. With your hands shape marble-sized pieces of dough into balls and arrange on the tray. Or you can press all of the mixture into a flat pan so that it is 2 cm thick. Cut it into squares.
5. Refrigerate for 30 minutes.

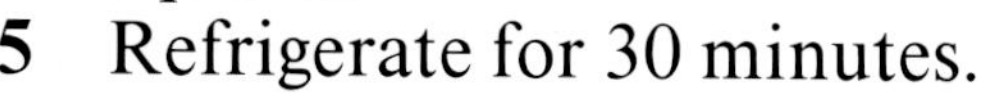

Bilby whiz-bang banana splits

Utensils:

dessert dish
knife
spoon
measuring spoons
chopping board

Ingredients:

1 banana
chocolate ice-cream
vanilla ice-cream
strawberry ice-cream
crushed nuts
whipped cream
hundreds and thousands
3 cherries
flavoured topping syrups such as:
pineapple
caramel
strawberry
chocolate

Method:

1 Peel the banana, cut in half lengthwise and place on dessert dish.
2 Put 1 scoop of vanilla ice-cream, 1 scoop of chocolate ice-cream and 1 scoop of strawberry ice-cream between the banana halves.
3 Pour 2 tablespoons of your favourite topping syrups over each scoop of ice-cream.
4 Top with whipped cream.
5 Sprinkle crushed nuts and hundreds and thousands over the whipped cream.
6 Top each scoop of ice-cream with a cherry and eat right away.

Bandicoot ginger biscuits

Utensils:

measuring cups and spoons
2 mixing bowls
2 wooden spoons
baking sheet
eggslice
cooling rack
plastic wrap
small bowl
piece of paper the size of your hand

Ingredients:

2½ cups plain flour
2 teaspoons bicarbonate of soda
1 teaspoon baking powder
1 teaspoon cinnamon
1 teaspoon ginger
1 teaspoon cloves
1 cup caster sugar
150 g soft butter
2 eggs
1 tablespoon golden syrup
1 cup extra sugar
butter

Method:

1 Butter the baking sheet by placing a small piece of butter onto a piece of paper. Rub the buttered paper over the inside of the baking sheet.

2 Put the butter into a mixing bowl and beat it by stirring quickly with a wooden spoon until it is smooth and creamy.

3 Now add the sugar and beat until the mixture is light and fluffy (about 50 times).

4 Add 1 egg at a time and beat well.

5 Stir in the golden syrup.

6 In the second mixing bowl measure the flour, soda, baking powder and spices. Using a clean spoon, stir these together 20 times so that the mixture is one colour.

7 Pour half of the dry mixture into the wet mixture and stir 20 times. Add the rest of the dry mixture and stir until it is smooth.

8 Ask an adult to cover the bowl with plastic wrap. Chill the dough in the refrigerator for 1 hour.

9 After 1 hour take the dough out of the refrigerator.

10 Pour the extra cup of sugar into a small bowl.

11 Wash and dry your hands. Rub a little butter onto the palms of your hands.

12 Using your hands, roll rounded teaspoonfuls of dough into balls.

13 Roll each ball in the sugar.

14 Place the balls on the baking sheet. Be sure to leave at least 4 cm around each one because they spread out as they cook.

15 Ask an adult to preheat the oven to 180°C.

16 When the oven is hot, ask an adult to put the baking sheet into the oven and cook the biscuits for 8 minutes.

17 After 8 minutes the biscuits should be golden brown. If they are, ask an adult to remove them from the oven. If not, let them cook for another 3 to 4 minutes.

18 Let the biscuits cool for 5 minutes. Then, using an eggslice, slide them onto a cooling rack until cold.

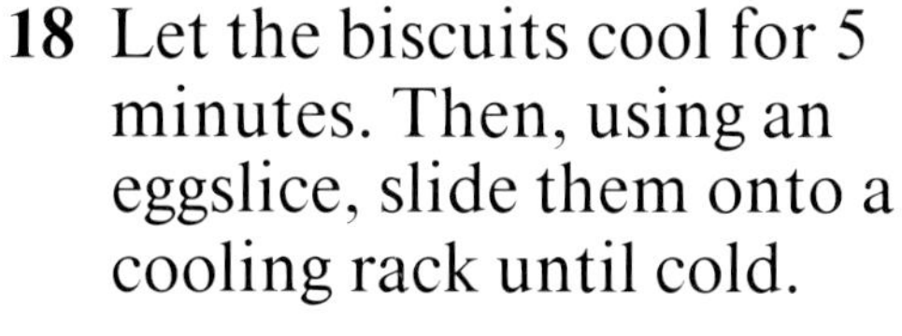